MAKE SHOW

poems by

Robin Lee

Finishing Line Press
Georgetown, Kentucky

MAKE SHOW

For lovers of poetry.

Copyright © 2017 by Robin Lee
ISBN 978-1-63534-319-9 First Edition
All rights reserved under International and Pan-American Copyright Conventions.
No part of this book may be reproduced in any manner whatsoever without written permission from the publisher, except in the case of brief quotations embodied in critical articles and reviews.

Publisher: Leah Maines

Editor: Christen Kincaid

Cover Art: Courtesy instrumental rock band SPURV.

Author Photo: Teresa Eckton

Cover Design: Robin Lee

Printed in the USA on acid-free paper.
Order online: www.finishinglinepress.com
            also available on amazon.com

> Author inquiries and mail orders:
> Finishing Line Press
> P. O. Box 1626
> Georgetown, Kentucky 40324
> U. S. A.

Table of Contents

In Situ   1

Disastrous Beauty   2

When Young   3

A Cooler Judgment   4

The Poem I Didn't Write About 911   5

A Spring Quinn   6

The Attic   7

Smooth Changes   9

Biography   10

Every Poem   11

Gallery   12

As Old As Possible   13

Under the Knife   14

Plenty of Money   16

Moonshine   17

Often Very Nervous   18

The Ocean   19

Placid Satisfaction   22

The Tiger Cub's Song   23

IN SITU

A message in

a bottle

A probe launched

into space

I press the Dark

for answers

The Dark laughs in

my face

DISASTROUS BEAUTY

She sat by his disastrous

beauty,

like living underneath a burning

glass.

He looked strong

indeed.

I was still conscious of

my youth.

Painfully conscious of my

youth.

The daisy of

the field at

sunrise.

WHEN YOUNG

When young the world
a mystery clouded,
mystery just beyond
proof.

Now search moments
minus lore, the sad
and factual
truth.

A COOLER JUDGMENT

I won't be quite absorbed.

He asked what I am afraid to extract.

I was sorry for reasons unsubstantial enough.

I was guided by you.

He must not be allowed to go back.

We must endeavor to form a cooler judgment.

He laughed as he ran his hand softly

before my lips (while I was

yet speaking).

THE POEM I DIDN'T WRITE ABOUT 911

The Poetry Group Director directs: write
a poem about 911, its impact and affect,
due next Wednesday's meeting.

To collar the event, fold it into my
orbit, two scant months after the
attack seems to me obscene.

And yet—driving west on Sir Francis
Drake off 101 towards my home I
approach Bon Air and ease

into the left turn lane,
onrushing traffic
to my right.

Waiting for the left turn light
I glimpse my rearview
mirror:

A glinting ray of sun, a cloud's
curious cast, three feet away cars
shoot past—

One of these metal containers of
gas will surely smash my gas
container.

A second's lapse neck
snaps mind
hushed.

Broken body rushed,
needlessly rushed,
to help.

It happens just like that.

A SPRING QUINN

Oh that was as a child or a

schoolboy said I laughing

in my turn.

So I understand said my

aunt rubbing her

nose—you'll

have to arrange our

contracts and bind

us to them.

I know you would have

told me (or at least

shed tears like

a child).

THE ATTIC

I must have been near seven, old
enough to be alone, because the house
was empty the afternoon I learned
about the attic.

I was playing in my room when I glanced
above the cupboard shelf. I saw a square of
painted wood set into an opening I had
not seen before.

Walking through familiar halls and rooms I
prepared my ascent. The known smells, the
carpet under my feet, my sure sense of
myself in this space mixed with my
anticipation.

I can't remember details but I must have
brought a chair in from the kitchen. Must
have pushed the clothes aside or removed
them. Placed the chair below the shelf and
climbed my uncertain way.

Once crouched on the landing I steadied
myself and caught my breath. Then rose slowly
on my knees to push the wood barrier up and
aside with my head and hands and
shoulders.

And rose into another world. Dark and cold and
deathly quiet. Pink surreal insulation, a jumble
of beams below and above, the still and cool unbreathed
air—all circled my small pool of light. Fast
afraid I made to leave.

But I did not leave. That within my home—a place
as close and warm as skin—that such an
abyss could exist held me still. The house I knew
for certain I really did
not know.

Even if I could not say it then, my house was
changed for me that day. The darkness never would
quite go away. And the darkness was there as
well, I knew, inside the body-home, inside
the world-home too.

I knew, or I began to know, it's all
an act of balance. That the certain shores
of house or life are not without their seas of
night. And that sea and shore together spin within
the larger night.

I descended from the attic into a different
light. Each sight our own for moments
only; each moment charged with flight. In
quiet company with the dark companion of
every full-lived life I waited for my parents
to return.

SMOOTH CHANGES

It would be preferred.

Of course it would be preferred.

"Have you observed any

gradual alteration?"

I had observed and

had wondered.

(I was filled with play I

assure you.)

We had gone so far, like

so many caged

sparrows.

BIOGRAPHY

If sometime, reading this or that
latest biography, you want a
start, try the following:

Go immediately to the section where
photographs of the subject's life are
grouped.

Observe a life compressed
into nine or ten pages
of pictures.

Pages one through three the writer
in swaddling clothes, in high school,
the flush of first success.

Pages four through six continued work,
his first and second wife, the settlements
of middle-age.

Pages seven through nine some travels,
some awards, pictured here with his adult
children, here in his last abode.

It is now twenty-three seconds since you
began to turn the pages. Our writer
is old now, diminished and gray.

Second twenty-four, page ten. For him,
as for us all, too soon, the
end.

EVERY POEM

Every poem a
letting
go

Ascent into we
do not
know

Frightful wind
swept scenes
indeed

What we resist
is what we
need

GALLERY

Wider than vision, ceiling to floor
tall, the flat black structure sprawls.

Closest to me wooden posts thick as my
thigh some slightly more some less than
knee high limn an undulant border. And
rising behind in ragged raked ascent more
posts. All painted an ungiving flat black.

Within this black, black cabinets are
found—some small as my hand some large as
my chest. Most of these cabinets are closed.
Those few somewhat ajar reveal still another
cabinet within, or empty black interior.

For all its fear it calls and calls.
Spurs slow self through cell-registered
thickets of old. Through caves unlit and cold.
And through, as well, the limitless cell of
black and of unblinking stars.

And back again to cabinets shut or cabinets
small ajar. Within our inside thicket dark we
often stumble, often fall. Then listen in the
soundless night for sounds of prey to
call.

AS OLD AS POSSIBLE

You know I was distinguished

in that little world (unless

it was a novel

effect). But do not be

alarmed by what

I say (a clumsy

laugh). We sat down together,

his head upon his desk,

least like himself:

he is as old as

possible.

UNDER THE KNIFE

I.

Blood spore shatter
splatter red eye near
die inside armies
under siege cells off-kilter
splinter split the ring of
masked assassins near our only
groping hope our help the tubes of
light fluorescent green the
deep and darker blood
machine the humming in our ears a
scream to sleep to sleep to
never dream

II.

Blocks of cities tumble a
child's impatient hand shards of
concrete stealing moonlight from the
street. Dark forbidding silence a
stranger's nearness fear
a gasping city grasping for the
way out exit entrance from the
wilding bullets flying to
the parting of the
flesh

III.

Spheres of crystal shatter the
snap of thread is
heard
the wheezing spinning circle hugs the
sword into its gut
Sun-shocked below we tell
ourselves we know the
movie's not yet over but the
house lights have
come
up

PLENTY OF MONEY

"Plenty of money in my pocket and

everyone spoils me."

"I understand."

"You may be surprised to hear no one

deserves to love."

She was so happy in herself, and

the other was happy too.

The next day is worse, and

worse. So he stepped between them,

as if by accident.

MOONSHINE

The night the night the
well water dances with
moon match glances,
water of the night.

Slowly slowly raise the pail,
drink this dancing moon
of light, then gaze into
the well of water,

water of the night.

OFTEN VERY NERVOUS

Another time I might have wanted

all his love and care.

I try in vain to recall how

I felt.

Do not be alarmed (I saw Jill

lift up her eyes)

You know as well as I do he is

often very nervous:

his hand his speech his

eyes—overcome by I need

not say.

THE OCEAN

There were the things he liked to do alone. And so
on this windless evening he walked all the way out
along the pier, right to the end. He listened to the
quiet ocean waves, observed no fishermen, no couples, no
solitary beings like himself. He was alone.

Standing there in his bathing suit the air felt close and
cool. Soon, he knew, his parents would be wondering
where he was. So without further waiting I drop my towel and
begin what I set out to
do.

I approach and climb the furthermost post that supports this
wooden structure. I look around. The cottages on the beach,
some now illumined with interior light, seem far away. The long
and dark and squeaking dock—a bridge between sure sand and
unknown ocean.

And the ocean itself. Stretching unbelievably away, the
gray clouds settling over. But it is time. Deep and slow I breathe
the air and then, a breath held within, jump from my height into the
ocean below. The air descent seems longer than it must have
been. A slow sensation flying. And then the sudden

sea embrace. A shock of cold spills over me I simply slip
its hold. I plunge down and down my eyes closed but still
I sense a falling off of light and water pressure mounting.
And then a slowing of my speed, a slow languor inside
opens...

Snap to alert with legs and arms and strain against the sea
uprushing. My falling stalled I pause, then begin to move up towards
air and light. Sensing small panic I aid my lung-filled lift by

kicking at the ocean, scraping at its sides. Then smash through its
surface gasping great chunks of air. I stroke my way back to the

water-blackened supports and tired climb my way up and over the rail to
the platform of the pier. If it was quiet before it seems more quiet
now. Swirled clouds shroud the pallor of the moon. A light wind
chills. Muscles already aching I climb the post again. Again several
deep breaths and relax; again I jump into the sea.

Down and down only this time the sudden sealed-off self the plunge into
another world seem somehow familiar. I drop deeper so deep the pressure
again increasing the light now fades away. My mother held me
close this once, once this close I know. My friends I send my world
towards, those I know I know I hold hands with my brothers make a
kindergarten reindeer I move my mouth in choir I do not sing do not sing
I sink am sinking think aloud must slow myself must go, must go....no,
again I know to slow the fall flail out legs and hands and once again
ascend an angel floating up to light and
breath...

And so again the sea's surface shatter and drink in light and heaving
gasps of air. Again swim to wooden pillars against which the ocean
falls and rises. And once again, wet and tired, scale the pier and
climb onto my post. Aware of looming last descent I stand and
deeply breathe.

And then with no delay leap high into the sky of night and for a moment
seem to fly then sunder living ocean-skin a sharpened falling
knife.

Down I plunge, faster than before, more intensely than before. The feel
of water flooding past me now a friend. I fall and fall. A speck
within the empty dark the ocean all around.

And now the place where before the urge to fall forever was suppressed.
I let it pass. I'm free I cry within my dream I am with all
surrounding.

And then the air within me slows my ocean-bottom journey. A final
floor of water feels my touch. And then this time without a move I
start towards the air. This one time the balance struck I feel the
intonation just. I rise and rise my closed eyes feel the sluice of
sea go by. A moment comes my need to breathe swells my lungs then falls
away. Riding tidal push through ocean womb perhaps this time to not
emerge. Ah yes the point the point at last as briny caverns closely
call to spiderman and thor as well the all-american-justice-league the
need to sink below the shore of now and here and less and more and will
the starlight sunburst sing of my and me and thought and thing this is
the measure full and lean that promised promises in dream. In dream I
find now what was sought I know I know the beauty dark the wish below
the final willing letting go the final letting letting go…

A last contraction and the ocean spits me foreign into air above.
Moon-bright in spite of night I flail my hapless way to wood and heave
my body to the pier. What am I doing here I dimly wonder as the dark
and darkling ocean call still softly in my ear.

PLACID SATISFACTION

I am getting lazy, like a stain

upon the quiet place I had

worked and played as

a boy.

I come to fall in love with a

fast-beating heart, and

said: "Won't you speak

to me?"

They looked very touching. Such

deep fondness—more than

I have ever

seen.

When I fall in love in earnest my

wonder is the wonder, the

mystery, the light's placid

satisfaction.

THE TIGER CUB'S SONG

Night in the jungle
so silent and still
sing hey lolly hey lolly ho
and whisper most closely
of things that are ghostly
of things one should not really know

Sing lolly hey lolly
sing hey lolly lolly
lolly hey lolly
hey lo

Now quietly creep
on the tips of your feet
lolly hey lolly hey lo
to the place where most rightly
you sing out most brightly
to the shine of the moon's silver glow

Sing lolly hey lolly
sing hey lolly lolly
lolly hey lolly
hey lo

Now stand in the light
of the noon of night
sing lolly hey lolly hey ho
and rise through the gloom
to the soul of the moon
and leave the jungle below

Sing lolly hey lolly
sing hey lolly lolly
lolly hey lolly
hey lo

Robin Lee has been writing poetry for many years and has been published in small magazines such as *Convolvulus* and the *Bay Guardian*. Professionally he works in film post-production as a Picture Editor. Robin's previous chapbooks, THE LIVE LONG DAY and RECKLESS SIMPLICITY, are available at finishinglinepress.com.

Robin lives in Marin County, California.

www.ingramcontent.com/pod-product-compliance
Lightning Source LLC
LaVergne TN
LVHW041519070426
835507LV00012B/1688